BUTTERFLIES

by Liza Jacobs

BLACKBIRCH®
PRESS

THOMSON
GALE

San Diego • Detroit • New York • San Francisco • Cleveland • New Haven, Conn. • Waterville, Maine • London • Munich

© 2003 by Blackbirch Press™. Blackbirch Press™ is an imprint of The Gale Group, Inc., a division of Thomson Learning, Inc.

Blackbirch Press™ and Thomson Learning™ are trademarks used herein under license.

For more information, contact
The Gale Group, Inc.
27500 Drake Rd.
Farmington Hills, MI 48331-3535
Or you can visit our Internet site at http://www.gale.com

Photographs © 1990 by Chang Yi-Wen

Cover photograph © Digital Stock

© 1995 by Chin-Chin Publications Ltd.

No. 274-1, Sec.1 Ho-Ping E. Rd., Taipei, Taiwan, R.O.C.
Tel: 886-2-2363-3486 Fax: 886-2-2363-6081

LIBRARY OF CONGRESS CATALOGING-IN-PUBLICATION DATA

Jacobs, Liza.
    Butterflies / by Liza Jacobs.
        v. cm. -- (Wild wild world)
    Includes bibliographical references.
    Contents: Butterflies -- Eating -- Stages.
    ISBN 1-5671-1811-9 (alk. paper)
    1. Butterflies--Juvenile literature. [1. Butterflies.] I. Title. II.
Series.

    QL544.2.J33 2003
    595.78'9--dc21

                                    2003001425

Printed in Taiwan
10 9 8 7 6 5 4 3 2 1

Table of Contents

About Butterflies 4

The Butterfly Body 6

Finding a Mate 8

Caterpillars 10

Eating and Growing .12

Colors and Patterns .14

Protected in a Case .16

Turning Into a Butterfly 18

Special Defenses 20

Butterflies and Moths 22

For More Information 24

Glossary 24

About Butterflies

Butterflies are one of the world's most-loved insects. There are almost 20,000 kinds of butterflies. They live in all parts of the world, except in cold polar areas. Butterflies are found in many dazzling, bright colors. Most butterflies feed on the nectar, or juice, of flowers.

The Butterfly Body

Butterflies have wings of different shapes, sizes, and colors. They use their wings to glide and fly through the air. Butterfly wings are covered in tiny scales that overlap like the shingles on a roof. Most butterflies have up to 500,000 scales on their wings! The scales are what give the wings their patterns and colors.

Like other insects, butterflies have compound eyes. Compound eyes are made up of hundreds of tiny eyes. This gives butterflies amazing eyesight. They can also see in many colors. This helps them find food and steer clear of enemies.

Butterflies have three pairs of long, thin legs. There are short hairs on their legs and feet that help butterflies taste! A butterfly chooses where to drink by walking on a plant!

Butterflies use a long thin tube to drink nectar from flowers. When a butterfly is not drinking, the tube is rolled up. The butterfly unrolls its tube when it needs to, sipping through it like a straw!

Finding a Mate

Butterflies have two antennae on their heads. The antennae are very sensitive and pick up sounds and smells. This is one way a male butterfly finds a mate. Many types of male butterflies do a kind of dance to attract a mate. The male flies above the female and quickly flutters his wings. If the female likes the male, she settles on to a plant. The male then follows her and they mate.

After mating, a female chooses a spot to lay her eggs. She looks for a safe place near a source of food. This way, her babies will have enough to eat when they hatch.

Caterpillars

The baby that hatches from a butterfly egg about a week later is called a caterpillar. It is also called a larva. When a caterpillar is ready to hatch, it eats a hole right through its eggshell. Then it wiggles out of the shell.

Caterpillars start to eat as soon as they are born. The first thing a caterpillar eats is its eggshell!

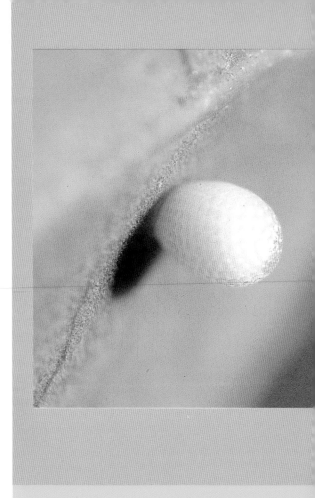

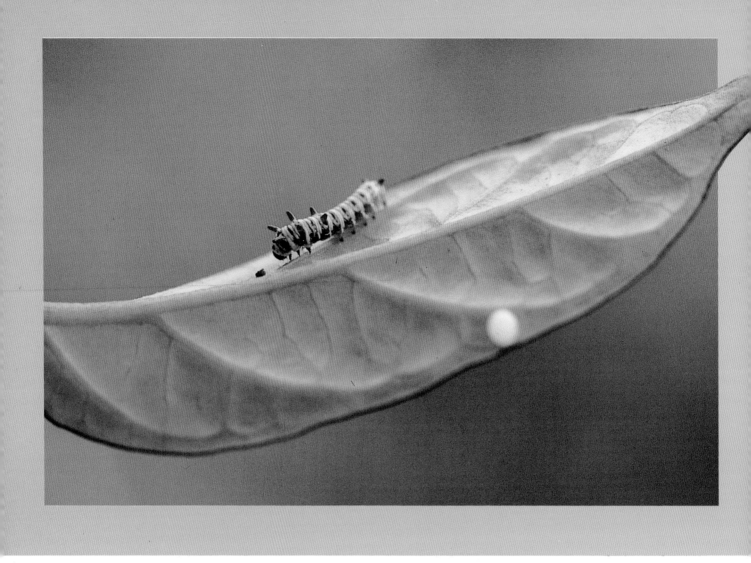

Eating and Growing

Caterpillars eat a lot! Most caterpillars eat leaves. They usually eat the type of leaf on which they hatch. They crawl from leaf to leaf, crunching up their food. Caterpillars have strong jaws for all that munching! They also have good senses of taste and smell that help them find food.

As a caterpillar eats, it grows. Soon, its skin becomes too tight for its body. Caterpillars shed their skin, or molt, a few times as their bodies grow.

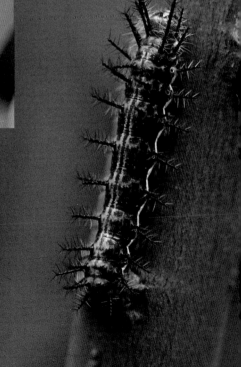

14

Colors and Patterns

Birds and other animals love to eat caterpillars. There are many different patterns, colors, and sizes of caterpillars. Their shapes and markings often help caterpillars escape attack. Some have patterns that confuse enemies (Look at the photo at the top left of page 14. Those are not the caterpillar's eyes—but they look like they are!). Others have shapes that look like horns and frighten off enemies. Still others can blend into the background, which makes them very hard to see.

Protected in a Case

When a caterpillar is finished growing, it is ready for its next stage of life. It looks for a safe place to stay still and not be bothered. It spins a small dot of silk that it uses to attach itself to a leaf or stem. The caterpillar molts one more time before becoming a pupa.

Just as caterpillars do, pupae have ways of protecting themselves. Some have false "eyespots" that confuse enemies. Some look like dead leaves or branches. Others are hard to see against the background of the leaves.

Although a pupa stays very still, there is a lot of activity going on inside the hardened pupa case!

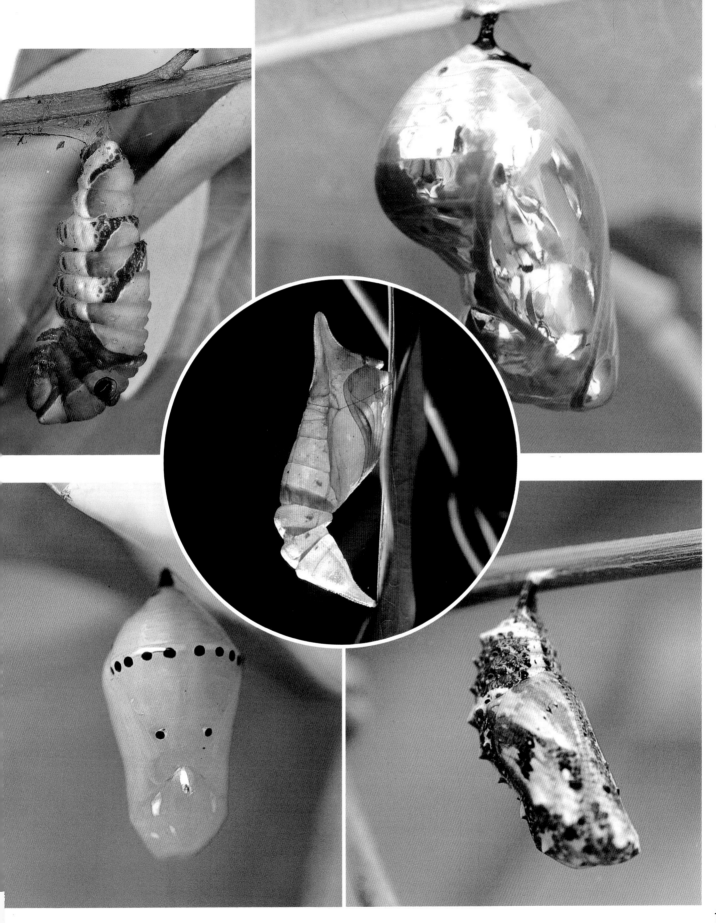

Turning Into a Butterfly

Inside its case, a pupa turns into a butterfly! Many parts of the caterpillar's body change into the adult form of a butterfly. Its compound eyes develop. So do its long legs and the tube through which the butterfly sucks nectar. When the butterfly is ready to come out,

its case splits open and the butterfly crawls out. At first, it does not look much like a butterfly. That is because its body is soft and its wings are folded and damp. Then the butterfly begins to stretch and spread its wings. In only about 30 minutes, the butterfly is ready to fly off in search of a flower.

Special Defenses

In each stage of life, butterflies have ways of protecting themselves from animals that want to eat them. Some adult butterflies blend into the background. Leaf butterflies look just like leaves when their wings are folded.

Other butterflies have false "eyespots." These are markings on their wings that look like large eyes. The spots are confusing—they make it hard to locate a butterfly's head. Eyespots also make a butterfly look like a much bigger, scarier animal. Instead of a butterfly being attacked, an enemy may run away in fear!

Butterflies and Moths

Butterflies are related to moths. They can be hard to tell apart, but there are some differences. Butterflies have knobs at the ends of their antennae and moths do not. Butterflies mainly fly during the day. Moths usually start to fly as the sun goes down.

When butterflies are resting, they usually have their wings upright. Moths generally fold them down. And butterflies are often more brightly colored than moths. Because they are so beautiful, butterflies are sometimes called the "jewels" of the insect world.

For More Information

Gibbons, Gail. *Monarch Butterfly.* New York: Holiday House, 1989.

Pascoe, Elaine. *Butterflies and Moths.* San Diego, CA: Blackbirch Press, 1997.

Stefoff, Rebecca. *Butterfly.* New York: Marshall Cavendish, 1997.

Glossary

compound eye an eye that has many lenses

molt to shed the outer skin or covering

pupa the life stage of a butterfly between the caterpillar and the adult